# the first five years

time flies when you're having fun...

To order additional copies of this book, contact:
Xlibris Corporation
1-888-795-4274
www.Xlibris.com
Orders@Xlibris.com

As we enter the 21st century, technology has given us wonderful information about how your child's brain grows from birth through the first years of life. The news is remarkable and encouraging. If you give your child time and attention, you can have a positive, permanent effect on your child's brain development. You will be your child's first teacher in the truest sense of the word.

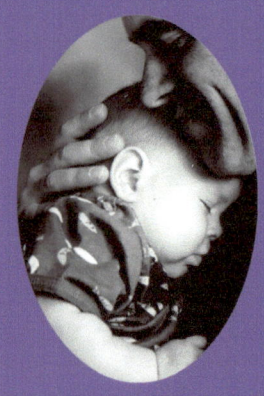

Children are born ready to learn and explore. From birth to three years of age, a child experiences the greatest amount of human growth and development. The quality of your child's life during the first five years will set the stage for future learning and success. The ages and stages described in this book can overlap, and of course, all children develop at different rates.

The challenge to parents might seem overwhelming, but the promising news is that you can easily provide the important experiences your child deserves. It doesn't require expensive materials, but it does require time and commitment. The attention you give your child now will reap the best reward: a child who is ready and eager to learn!

*The biggest surprise is . . . small things can make a big difference. This book was designed with that in mind.*

# contents

0-3 Months
3-6 Months

6-9 Months
9-12 Months

12-18 Months
18-24 Months

24-36 Months

3 Years

4-5 Years

Rock-a-bye-baby on the tree top.

| 0-3 Months 3-6 Months | 6-9 Months 9-12 Months | 12-18 Months 18-24 Months | 24-36 Months | 3 Years | 4-5 Years |

## 0-3 Months

### Stimulating the Senses

#### Visual Stimulation
Babies can see clearly at birth. It is important to have mobiles, posters and bright colors he can look at easily.

#### Auditory Stimulation
Babies enjoy hearing their caretaker's voice. Talk and sing to him in a soothing voice. Play jingle bells, shake rattles or other gentle-sounding instruments.

#### Tactile Stimulation
Babies enjoy and need touch. Blankets with satin edges, soft/smooth stuffed animals and feathers provide pleasant tactile experiences for him.

## 3-6 Months

### Stimulating the Senses

#### Visual Stimulation
Babies continue to expand their awareness through the senses. Colorful objects and crib mirrors are some ways you can help her develop and refine her sensory experiences.

#### Auditory/Tactile Stimulation
Babies enjoy rattles and squeaky toys. This is the beginning of "first conversations," as you respond to her first attempts at face-to-face "talking" (baby sounds). Play soothing music, and include singing voices. Read short board books or fabric books to her. Babies also enjoy small, stuffed animal toys and other soft toys to play with.

### Suggested Book List

#### 0-3 Months
Any book, magazine, newspaper or simple rhymes you read would be fine.

#### 3-6 Months
- *Play Rhymes*, by Marc Brown
- *Tomie dePaola's Mother Goose*, by Tomie dePaola
- *Read-Aloud Rhymes for the Very Young*, by Jack Prelutsky

# Journal entries

# Journal entries

What does the cow say?

6-9 Months
9-12 Months

12-18 Months
18-24 Months

24-36 Months

3 Years

4-5 Years

## 9-12 Months

### 6-9 Months

#### Stimulating the Senses/Language Development

##### Visual/Tactile
Your baby is able to move on his own. Dedicate a drawer easily accessible to him and fill it with favorite toys, clothes and books. Include wooden spoons, pots, and safe kitchen objects. Add something new to discover every day or two.

##### Auditory/Language Development
This is a good time to grasp the meaning of words. Recite nursery rhymes to your baby. Name objects in the environment (light, table, book, bed, etc.). Continue reading to him. Point out familiar objects in books that have large, clear illustrations. For example: Say, "Look at the baby with the rattle. Can you see the rattle?"

#### Sensory/Motor Skills
Babies enjoy exploring their environment and the objects in it. Provide toys to put together and take apart. Include toys that fit inside one another. Pop-up toys, balls, and jack in-the-box toys are all enjoyable for her. Encourage fine motor development by providing finger foods, and allowing her to pull off her shoes and socks. Give her a spoon to eat with.

#### Language Development
Babies begin to link the understanding of speech with ideas. Find books that have ideas in them such as: in/out; up/down; hot/cold. Continue to read to your baby and let her choose books for you to read. Include books about daily life (bathing, playing outdoors). Pop-up books and pull-tab books are enjoyable for her. This is also the beginning of real conversation. Parents should respond to their baby's attempt at language. You might ask, "What does the cow say?" "What does the cat say?"

#### Suggested Book List

**6-9 Months**
- *Spot's Toys*, by Eric Hill
- *What is It?*, by Tana Hoban
- *Pat the Bunny*, by Dorothy Kunhardt
- *Dressing*, by Helen Oxenbury
- *The Blanket*, by John Burningham
- *The Helen Oxenbury Nursery Rhyme Book*, by Brian Alderson and Helen Oxenbury (illustrator)
- *Eye Winker, Tom Tinker, Chin Chopper: A Collection of Musical Finger Plays*, by Tom Glazer
- *Have You Seen My Duckling?*, by Nancy Tafuri

**9-12 Months**
- *More More More Said the Baby*, by Vera B. Williams
- *Where's Spot?*, by Eric Hill
- *Goodnight Moon*, by Margaret Wise Brown
- *Clap Hands*, by Helen Oxenbury
- *The Tub People*, by Pam Conrad
- *Color Zoo*, by Lois Ehlert
- *I Love Colors*, by Margaret Miller
- *Baby Food*, by Margaret Miller

# Journal entries

# Journal entries

Do you want a drink of water?

# 12-18 Months

## Language Development

Encourage your child's attempts to be understood. Give your child your undivided attention and listen to what he is saying. Talk about what he seems to want to say. For example, when he points to a sink, respond by asking, "Are you thirsty?" "Do you want a drink of water?" Say words for feelings and actions: "Grandpa is funny, isn't he?" "I saw you get the ball." Match what your child is doing with words: "First put on one shoe. Now put on the other shoe." Sing songs together. Recite nursery rhymes and poems.

## Reading Readiness

Your child's attention span is short. Read throughout the day, rather than in one, long period of time. Let him know you think books and reading are fun. Let him turn the pages when you are reading, and point out objects in the pictures. Smile, change your tone of voice and make faces when you read to help him understand and enjoy stories.

# 18-24 Months

## Language Development

Language abilities are blossoming. A child acquires approximately one word every two hours. Parents should use "Please" and "Thank You" in conversation. It is important to use proper sentence structure. Give simple directions. For example: "Go to your room and get your shoes." Always praise your child for following the direction. Talk to your child and tell her what you are doing: "I'm fixing the leak in the sink." "I'm cutting the grass."

## Reading Readiness

Read to your child every day. Read the same books many times and add new ones. Choose books with repeated phrases, rhyming patterns, and songs. Include books with counting patterns in them and then count the stairs as you climb or count the buttons on a sweater. Provide toys that are related to books and reading: magnetic numbers and letters, sponge letters and alphabet puzzles are good examples. Find a special place in the house and the yard for exploration. Have digging toys available. Play simple games such as hide and seek. Large piece puzzles and ride-on toys are good for this age.

## Suggested Book List

### 12-18 Months
- *Bedtime Rhymes*, by Carol Thompson
- *DK Read & Listen: Playtime Rhymes*, by Priscilla Lamont
- *Corduroy*, by Don Freeman
- *Peter's Chair,* by Ezra Jack Keats
- *The Snowy Day*, by Ezra Jack Keats
- *Rosie's Walk*, by Pat Hutchins

### 18-24 Months
- *Richard Scarry's Best Mother Goose Ever*, by Richard Scarry
- *Jack Kent's Book of Nursery Tales*, by Polly Berends
- *The Tale of Peter Rabbit*, by Beatrix Potter
- *The Runaway Bunny*, by Margaret Wise Brown
- *The Little Red Hen*, by Byron Barton

# Journal entries

# Journal entries

Yesterday we played outside.

## 24-36 Months

### Language Development

Children learn about language by watching, listening and imitating adults. Talk about the past, present, and future: "Yesterday we played outside." "Today (or now) we are going to read a book." "Tomorrow we will be going to the store." Look through photo albums. Pick out people and talk about family relationships: "That's my daddy's brother." Talk about real life experiences. Review the happenings of the day. Also ask your child what he might want to do for the day. Allow your child to explore on his own. Do not overly structure your child's day.

### Reading/Writing Readiness

Have a special time or times each day to read. Bedtime is always a good opportunity. Take trips to the library. Let your child read along with you. Have him say the parts that repeat throughout the story. Read with a lot of enthusiasm. Use different voices for characters and their feelings. Be patient if the child interrupts as you read. Answer questions about the story and discuss how things relate to his experiences. Encourage him to stop and look at the pictures. Ask questions about the pictures in the book: "What are the boys and girls doing?" Let him draw pictures of the characters in the stories. Always have crayons and paper available for spontaneous pictures, and have him tell you about the picture. Remember, there is never a right or wrong way to draw a picture. When you are out and about, read signs, grocery store items, and other things you see.

To expand your child's thinking skills, have him help you sort by putting groceries away. Explain why some things go in the freezer or refrigerator. Talk about how these items are the same or different. Sort and match objects: buttons, socks, shoes. Encourage building simple puzzles, playing in the sandbox, and using housekeeping or kitchen props to pretend with.

### Suggested Book List

#### 24-36 Months

- *Clifford The Big Red Dog*, by Norman Bridwell
- *The Very Hungry Caterpillar*, by Eric Carle
- *Brown Bear, Brown Bear, What Do You See?*, by Bill Martin, Jr.
- *Wheels on the Bus*, by Raffi
- *Wait Till the Moon Is Full*, by Margaret Wise Brown
- *Stellaluna*, by Jannell Cannon
- *Millions of Cats*, by Wanda Gag

# Journal entries

# Journal entries

Why are you digging in the dirt?

## 3 Years

### Language Development

Children begin to use short, simple sentences. They ask many questions. Give specific answers. "Why" questions tell you your child is growing up. She wants to add more information to her world: "Why are you digging in the dirt?" "Because I'm going to plant flowers for the garden." Help your child describe how things look and feel: "That's a big, brown dog." "Your shirt is soft."

### Reading/Writing Readiness

This is a good time to encourage your child's love of books. Help her understand they are an important part of her life. Make frequent visits to the library. When you are reading alphabet books, point out letters that appear in her name. Find the letter her favorite cereal begins with. Write down stories your child tells you. Read them back to her. Encourage her to draw about the things she sees and things you read about. Continue to have plenty of materials available to draw and write with.

### Suggested Book List

**3 Years**
- **Mooncake**, by Frank Asch
- **Are You My Mother?**, by P.D. Eastman
- **We're Going on a Bearhunt**, by Michael Rosen
- **The Three Bears**, by Paul Galdone
- **Blueberries for Sal**, by Robert McCloskey
- **The Napping House**, by Audrey Wood
- **Curious George**, by H.A. Rey
- **The Cat in the Hat**, by Dr. Seuss

# Journal entries

We saw lions then we went to the zoo

## 4-5 Years

### Language Development

Have conversations with your child. Start a conversation with a question using "What do you think?" or "What if . . ." Television watching can be used as an opportunity to talk to your child about what he sees and hears. Visit interesting places and take your child along when you do errands. Talk about what you see and do.

### Reading/Writing Readiness

Children are beginning to understand how books "work." Point out details in pictures. Begin pointing to the start of each word as you read. This will help your child become aware that we read books left to right. When he interrupts while you read to ask questions, add more information and relate it to his experience: "Look at those lions. We saw lions when we went to the zoo." Share ways to find information in the newspaper, how to read a recipe or what the weather will be like. Choose books about families like yours and people from your culture and background.

Help your child understand that the things he says can be written down. Let him see you writing. Tell him you are writing a letter to someone or making a list. Ask him if he would like to add an idea of his own to the letter or list. Have materials available for him to do his own writing. Show him where to start. Don't worry if you can't read what he has written. Ask him to read it when he is finished. You may be surprised at what he "reads" to you!

### Suggested Book List

#### 4-5 Years

- **Sylvester and the Magic Pebble**, by William Steig
- **The Story of Ferdinand**, by Munro Leaf
- **Make Way for Ducklings**, by Robert McCloskey
- **Chicka Chicka Boom Boom**, by Bill Martin Jr.
- **If You Give a Mouse a Cookie**, by Laura Joffe Numeroff
- **Where the Wild Things Are**, by Maurice Sendak
- **I Read Signs**, by Tana Hoban
- **The Mitten**, by Jan Brett
- **Tikki Tikki Tembo**, by Arlene Mosel
- **Lyle, Lyle, Crocodile**, by Bernard Waber
- **The Snowman**, by Raymond Briggs

# Journal entries

# Journal entries

# Book List

Asch, Frank. *Mooncake.* New York: Aladdin Paperbacks, 1999.

Alderson, Brian and Oxenbury, Helen (illustrator). *The Helen Oxenbury Nursery Rhyme Book.* New York: William Morrow & Co., 1990.

Barton, Byron. *The Little Red Hen.* New York: HarperCollins, 1997.

Bender, Robert. *The A to Z Beastly Jamboree.* New York: Dutton, 1996.

Berends, Polly. *Jack Kent's Book of Nursery Tales.* New York: Random House, 1970.

Brett, Jan. *The Mitten.* New York: Putnam, 1989.

Bridwell, Norman. *Clifford The Big Red Dog.* New York: Scholastic, 1997.

Briggs, Raymond. *The Snowman.* New York: Random House, 1989.

Brown, Marc. *Play Rhymes.* New York: Puffin Books, 1993.

Brown, Margaret Wise. *Goodnight Moon.* New York: HarperCollins, 1991.

Brown, Margaret Wise. *The Runaway Bunny.* New York: HarperCollins, 1991.

Brown, Margaret Wise. *Wait Till the Moon Is Full.* New York: HarperCollins, 1989.

Burningham, John. *The Blanket.* New York: Candlewick Press, 1996.

Cannon, Janell. *Stellaluna.* San Diego: Harcourt, 1993.

Carle, Eric. *The Very Hungry Caterpillar.* New York: Philomel, 2000.

Conrad, Pam. *The Tub People.* New York: HarperTrophy, 1999.

Crowther, Robert. *My Pop-up Surprise ABC.* New York: Orchard Books, 1997.

dePaola, Tomie. *Tomie dePaola's Mother Goose.* New York: Putnam, 1985.

Eastman, P.D. *Are You My Mother?* New York: Random House, 1984.

Ehlert, Lois. *Color Zoo.* New York: HarperCollins, 1997.

Ehlert, Lois. *Eating the Alphabet: Fruits and Vegetables from A to Z.* New York: Harcourt Brace & Company, 1989.

Freeman, Don. *Corduroy.* New York: Viking Press, 1985.

Gag, Wanda. *Millions of Cats.* New York: Putnam, 1996.

Galdone, Paul. *The Three Bears.* New York: Scholastic, 1975.

Glazer, Tom. *Eye Winker, Tom Tinker, Chin Chopper: A Collection of Musical Finger Plays.* New York: Doubleday, 1992.

Hague, Kathleen. *Alphabears: An ABC Book.* New York: Henry Holt, 1984.

Hill, Eric. *Spot's Toys.* New York: Putnam, 1984.

Hill, Eric. *Where's Spot?* New York: Putnam, 2000.

Hoban, Tana. *I Read Signs.* New York: Pearson Learning, 1987.

Hoban, Tana. *What is It?* New York: William Morrow & Co., 1985.

Hutchins, Pat. *Rosie's Walk.* New York: Simon & Schuster, 1968.

Johnson, Stephen T. *Alphabet City.* New York: Viking Press, 1995.

Keats, Ezra Jack. *Peter's Chair.* New York: Viking Press, 1998.

Keats, Ezra Jack. *The Snowy Day.* New York: Viking Press, 1998.

Kunhardt, Dorothy. *Pat the Bunny.* New York: Golden Books, 2001.

Laidlaw, Ken. **The Amazing I Spy ABC.** New York: Dial Books, 1996.

Lamont, Priscilla. **DK Read & Listen: Playtime Rhymes.** New York: DK Publishing, 2000.

Leaf, Munro. **The Story of Ferdinand.** New York: Viking Press, 1987.

Martin, Bill, Jr. **Brown Bear, Brown Bear, What Do You See?** New York: Henry Holt & Co., 1996.

Martin, Bill, Jr. and Archambault, John. **Chicka Chicka Boom Boom.** New York: Simon & Schuster, 1991.

McCloskey, Robert. **Blueberries for Sal.** New York: Viking Press, 1987.

McCloskey, Robert. **Make Way for Ducklings.** New York: Viking Press, 1969.

McDonald, Suse. **Alphabatics.** New York: Aladdin Paperbacks, 1986.

Miller, Margaret. **Baby Food.** New York: Little Simon, 2000.

Miller, Margaret. **I Love Colors.** New York: Little Simon, 1999.

Mosel, Arlene. **Tikki Tikki Tembo.** New York: Henry Holt & Co., 1988.

Numeroff, Laura Joffe. **If You Give a Mouse a Cookie.** New York: HarperCollins, 1985.

Oxenbury, Helen. **Clap Hands.** New York: Little Simon, 1999.

Oxenbury, Helen. **Dressing.** New York: Little Simon, 2000.

Potter, Beatrix. **The Tale of Peter Rabbit.** New York: Frederick Warne, 1987.

Prelutsky, Jack. **Read-Aloud Rhymes for the Very Young.** New York: Random House, 1997.

Raffi. **Wheels on the Bus.** New York: Crown Publishing, 1998.

Rey, H.A. **Curious George.** Boston: Houghton Mifflin, 1994.

Rosen, Michael. **We're Going on a Bearhunt.** New York: Simon & Schuster, 1997.

Scarry, Richard. **Richard Scarry's Best Mother Goose Ever.** New York: Golden Books, 1970.

Sendak, Maurice. **Where the Wild Things Are.** New York: HarperCollins, 1988.

Seuss, Dr. **The Cat in the Hat.** New York: Random House, 1997.

Steig, William. **Sylvester and the Magic Pebble.** New York: Simon & Schuster, 1989.

Tafuri, Nancy. **Have You Seen My Duckling?** New York: Viking Press, 1986.

Thompson, Carol. **Bedtime Rhymes.** New York: Little Barron's, 1999.

Tucker, Sian. **A Is for Astronaut.** New York: Little Simon, 1995.

Waber, Bernard. **Lyle, Lyle, Crocodile.** Boston: Houghton Mifflin, 1973.

Williams, Vera B. **More More More Said the Baby.** New York: William Morrow & Co., 1990.

Wood, Audrey. **The Napping House.** San Diego: Harcourt, 1984.

www.ingramcontent.com/pod-product-compliance
Lightning Source LLC
Chambersburg PA
CBHW060810290526
45792CB00005BA/1590